Paddle to Perfection!

with 181 visual aids

Aquatics Unlimited, Inc.
Boston, MA

Written by Mark B. Solomon.
Edited by Gary B. Solomon.

Black & white photography by Robert Tannenbaum.
Color flat water photography by Amy L. Solomon.
Color white water photography by Robert Tannenbaum.
Graphic artwork by Mark and Gary Solomon.

Flat water shot on location at
Camp Avoda, Middleboro, MA.

Flat water canoes provided by
Great Canadian Canoe Company, Sutton, MA.

White water shot on location on the
Androscoggin River, Errol, NH.

White water canoes provided by
Mad River Canoe, Waitsfield, VT.

Published by Aquatics Unlimited, Inc., Boston, MA.

Printed by Arcadia Press, West Bridgewater, MA.

Distributed by ICS Books, Inc.
1370 E. 86th Place, Merrillville, IN 46410 (800) 541-7323

Preface

The four sections of <u>Paddle to Perfection!</u> are individual learning units. The student learns a complete skill set in each section: canoe knowledge tools, practical skills, and paddling strokes. Each section builds upon the skills taught in the previous section. Review questions and answers allow the student to measure his or her learning progress.

Crew Section:
The Crew Section is designed to educate the student in flat water canoeing fundamentals. At the end of the Crew Section, the crew member and a partner should be able to paddle the canoe on a straight course and spin the canoe with ease!

Captain Section:
The Captain Section is designed to educate the student in advanced flat water canoeing issues. At the end of the Captain Section, the captain and a partner should be able to handle most flat water situations, and two captains should be able to control the canoe through any flat water paddling exercise! (All paddling strokes used for tandem flat water and white water paddling have been learned at the end of the Captain Section.)

Solo Section:
The Solo Section is designed to educate the student in solo paddling philosophies. At the end of the Solo Section, the solo paddler should be able to efficiently paddle a canoe alone through the use of proper seating location, modified tandem paddling strokes, and strokes specific to solo paddling!

River Team Section:
The River Team Section is designed to educate the student in white water river safety issues and paddling techniques. At the end of the River Team Section, a river team, under supervision of an experienced white water paddling leader, should be able to safely navigate their way down a class 2 white water river!

We dedicate this book to our parents, Barbara and Leonard Solomon, for providing us the opportunity to spend our childhood years at summer camp, for being our education role models, and for being so supportive throughout the entire *Paddle to Perfection!* project.

Table of Contents

Table of Contents

Table of Contents

Welcome aboard! Today we'll be learning the finer points of canoeing: everything from canoe nomenclature and coordinating strokes to the stationary cross draw and eddy turns!

Figure 1. Your canoeing instructors, Mark and Gary

That's right, Mark. This will be an exciting day on the water, as always. We'll be covering all that you just mentioned and much more in our outdoor classroom. Don't worry if Mark's words sounded foreign; by the end of this course, we'll all be speaking the same language.

Figure 2. White water paddling

Crew Introduction
* safety
* use of PFD
* recommended safety equipment

Safety is just another word for common sense, and in canoeing, like all watersports, *one must always be prepared for the unexpected.*

Figure 3. Unexpected event

I'm helping Lara put on a Type II PFD, or personal flotation device. We listen for the click, adjust the fit, and tie the top in a bow.

Figure 4. Listen for the click and adjust the fit

10

Figure 5. Secure the PFD

Always be sure that you are wearing a PFD correctly rated for your weight. This information can be found on the Coast Guard **approval label** located on the rear of the PFD.

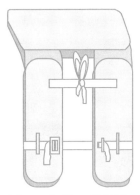

The difference between Lara's **Type II PFD** and Gary's **Type III PFD** is head support. The Type II PFD is designed to keep the wearer's breathing passages clear of the water if the wearer should become unconscious.

Figure 6. Type II PFD

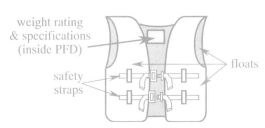

weight rating & specifications (inside PFD)

floats

safety straps

Figure 7. Type III PFD

Experienced paddlers often wear a Type III PFD because it provides more movement freedom than the Type II PFD. The decision to use a Type III PFD or a Type II PFD should be based on the user's boating experience, swimming ability, and weather and water conditions.

11

Maintain the PFD's safety qualities by hanging it to dry, keeping it clean, and especially *not* using it as a seat cushion. *Be good to your PFD; it may just save your life.*

Figure 8. Unconscious boater with Type II PFD

Wearing **shoes** with non-skid soles protects feet from injury and reduces the likelihood of slipping on wet surfaces. Always wear a high numbered **sunscreen** correct for your skin type.

Figure 9. Shoes with non-skid soles   *Figure 10. Sunscreen*

Sunglasses with UV protection are a must to protect the eyes.

Figure 11. Wear sunglasses

Wearing appropriate clothing will make our boating experience more comfortable, but good judgement in this regard also protects us from medical conditions, such as **sunstroke**, **heat exhaustion**, and **hypothermia**. We recommend seeking current medical literature on the dangers which can result from prolonged exposure to the elements.

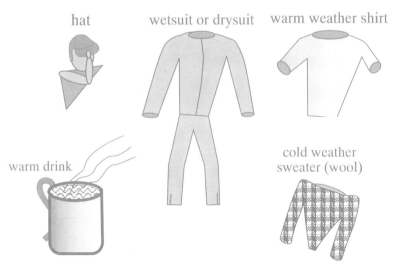

Figure 12. Appropriate clothing and drinks

The required and recommended **safety equipment** is as important as proper protection from the elements. We should have **audible**

13

Figure 13. Audible, visual signals

and **visual distress signals** available on the craft. These items are also important for safety: **bailer**, **spare PFD**, **extra line**, **heaving line**, **spare paddle**, and **anchor**. Of course, remember your **first aid kit**. *Be informed of current local waterway regulations.*

Common sense suggests knowing your limits. Recognize your abilities, be aware of other craft, shallow water, rocks, and other obstructions.

Figure 14. Spare paddle

Always inform someone on shore that you are on the water, and *be sure to have proper supervision.* And, in case of an emergency, be prepared to use the audible and visual distress signals.

Figure 15. Other recommended safety equipment

14

Crew Tools

* **nomenclature**
* **choosing a paddle**

Tools are important for getting a job done. Canoe **nomenclature**, or names of parts of the canoe, is a paddler's most important communication tool. Let's review some canoe nomenclature basics...

We'll begin with the general parts of the **canoe**. The front of the canoe is known as the **bow**, and the back of the canoe is called the **stern**. The side to paddler's left is referred to as the **port** - note four letters in port and left - and the **starboard** is the side to paddler's right.

Figure 16. Basic canoe nomenclature

Some specific canoe parts are the **gunnels**, or tops of the sides, the bow and stern **seats**, the **thwarts**, which are the horizontal bars used to hold the canoe's shape, the **breastplates**, found at the bow and stern, and the **bangplates** which protect the ends of the canoe. A **keel** travels between the bow and stern; it is used to hold two halves of some canoe types together.

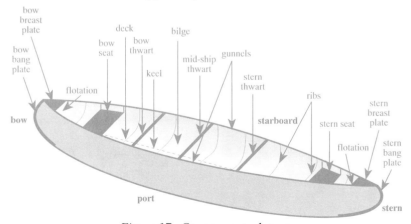

Figure 17. Canoe nomenclature

Canoe **paddle** nomenclature is also useful when communicating with other paddlers. The piece at the top is called the **grip** or **handle**. The **shaft** refers to the pole linking the grip to the **blade**. The **neck** or **throat** refers to the shaft just above the blade. The flat parts of the blade are called the **faces**. The sides of the blade are called the **edges**, and the end of the blade is the **tip**.

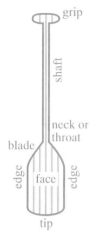

Figure 18. Paddle nomenclature

Now that we know paddle nomenclature, we can more easily discuss three methods for **choosing the correct paddle size**. To choose a paddle that is the correct size, we can:

- place the tip on our shoe; the grip should be between our chin and nose.
- curl our fingers around the tip and grip; our arms should be extended with elbows straight.
- hold the paddle over our head - one hand below the grip and one on the neck; our elbows should make rectangular bends.

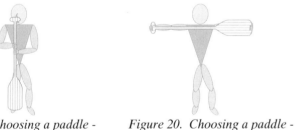

Figure 19. Choosing a paddle -   *Figure 20. Choosing a paddle -*
chin and nose   *arms straight*

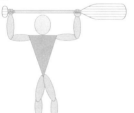

Figure 21. Choosing a paddle - rectangular bend

16

Crew Practical

* portaging
* boarding and deboarding
* using the paddle

Because canoes are often kept out of the water when not in use, the canoe crew member should be familiar with a method to **portage**, or carry, a canoe.

Figure 22. Breast plate carry

A good technique is the **breast and bang plate carry**. This tends to be an easy two-person carry, *especially for children.*

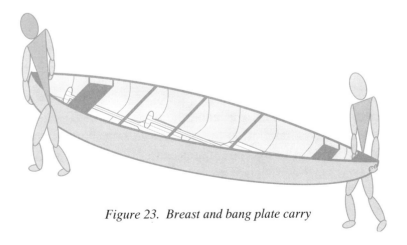

Figure 23. Breast and bang plate carry

17

Figure 24. Suitcase carry

The **suitcase carry** offers a change of pace, which may be desirable during a long portage. Some paddlers find the **reverse grip carry** makes for a comfortable method of portaging.

Figure 25. Reverse grip carry   Figure 26. Proper boarding position

Boarding and **deboarding** a canoe should be regarded as a skill. We *stow* our paddles flat on the deck, *hold* onto both gunnels, *place* the first foot across the canoe's center line, *step* behind our hands, and *shift* our weight to help keep the canoe balanced. Holding both gunnels while moving to a seat keeps body weight low for canoe stability. Once seated, our partner may then board the floating craft in the same fashion, and we are ready to go.

Figure 27. Stow paddles

Figure 28. Hold gunnels, stay low

Before we begin paddling, let's quickly discuss how one **holds the paddle**. When paddling on starboard, the right hand, or starboard hand holds the neck, and the left or port hand holds the grip. The hand on the neck is referred to as the **control hand**; the

Figure 29. Hold the neck with control hand

hand on the grip is referred to as the **grip hand**. The thumb on the grip hand should be placed under the hook if the grip is so equipped. To change paddling sides, the paddle is simply passed between hands such that *the blade tip always points downward.*

Figure 30. Curl fingers over grip

Figure 31. Tip always points downward

Crew Strokes

- forward power stroke
- reverse power stroke
- feathering
- stopping the canoe
- turning mechanics
- sweeps
- paddling a straight course

The **forward power stroke**, or forward stroke, is the most basic paddling stroke used to make the canoe move forward. When performing the power stroke, we move the blade from bow to stern using a hand-over-hand motion.

Figure 32. Extend blade forward

Hand-over-hand motion means that the grip hand will pass directly over the control hand so the blade passes vertically through the water.

Figure 33. Hand-over-hand paddling motion

We will define **power face** as the blade face which *pushes* the water during the power stroke. The other face is known as the **reverse face**.

Figure 34. Power face pushes water

The **recovery** portion of the power stroke begins when the blade reaches a horizontal position relative to the water's surface. We simply *slice* or **feather the blade** through the air with the power face up as the blade travels back toward the bow in preparation for the next forward power stroke. Feathering during the recovery saves us energy, which is better used during the water contact portion of our stroke.

Figure 35. Feather during power stroke recovery

A power stroke is less tiring if the control arm is kept straight and most of the energy comes from the "push" or "punch" of the grip arm. In fact, 80% of a normal power stroke should come from the push of the grip arm. These arm movements should lead to a smooth and natural rotation of the shoulders.

Figure 36. Power stroke - push with grip arm and rotate shoulders

The power stroke is more effective the longer the blade strokes vertically through the water. To get the blade to pass vertically through the water during the power stroke, paddlers use the hand-over-hand method, which requires a slight lean over the side of the canoe. But, because bow and stern paddlers *always* paddle on opposite sides, the canoe remains balanced.

Figure 37. Slight lean for hand-over-hand paddling

23

Paddlers can **stop the canoe's** forward momentum by simply placing the blade vertically into the water with the reverse face 90° to the direction of movement. Paddlers must hold their paddles tightly because of the force on their blades while bringing the canoe to a halt.

Figure 38. Stopping the canoe

The **reverse power stroke** is used to make the canoe go backward. The paddle motion during the reverse power stroke is performed just as it sounds: a reverse motion of the forward power stroke. Notice that during the reverse power stroke recovery, the blade's reverse face naturally faces the sky.

Figure 39. Reverse power stroke

We should now be proficient in making the canoe go forward and backward, but we also need the ability to turn the canoe to head back to shore. The strokes good crew members use to spin the canoe are called **sweeps**. Before learning sweeps, let's first understand the mechanics behind making the canoe spin.

pivot point

In tandem paddling, the center of the canoe is generally the pivot point about which the canoe spins. The farther away from the pivot point a sideward force is placed on the canoe, in this case our paddle blades pushing water, the more effect the force will have in making the canoe spin. A good analogy is a revolving glass door. The **revolving glass door** spins more easily when pushed on farther away from where the doors meet in the center.

Figure 40. Revolving glass door analogy

In canoeing, with every action, there is an equal and opposite reaction. So, if we sweep, or arc our blade smoothly through the water in a clockwise direction, that end of the canoe will move counter-clockwise. If we sweep our blade counter-clockwise, that end of the canoe will move clockwise. Based on the **canoe turning principle** just discussed, the bow paddler should lean forward and

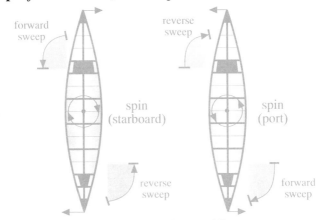

Figure 41. Sweeps - bow paddling port

the stern paddler should lean backward when performing sweeps to move the blades farther from the canoe's pivot point. The shaded areas represent the regions in which forward and reverse sweeps produce the most turning power.

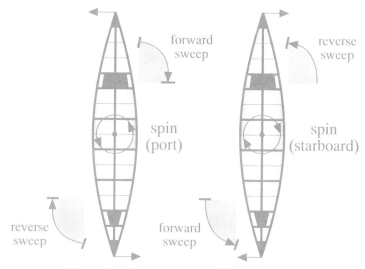

Figure 42. Sweeps - bow paddling starboard

Paddlers can spin the canoe by employing a combination of forward and reverse sweep strokes. The **sweep stroke combinations** determine spinning to port or starboard. A forward sweep on starboard by the bow paddler and reverse sweep on port by the stern paddler results in the canoe's spinning to port. Spinning to starboard is left as an exercise for the student!

Figure 43. Reverse sweep recovery

Figure 44. Reverse sweep in stern

Figure 45. Pivot (spin) the canoe using sweeps

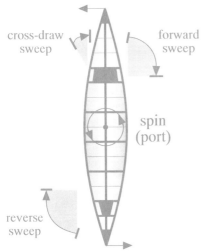

cross-draw
sweep

forward
sweep

spin
(port)

reverse
sweep

Figure 46. Cross draw sweep

If the *bow paddler* wishes to make the forward sweep more powerful, he or she can extend this sweep by performing what is known as the **cross draw sweep**. The blade should be placed about 30° across the imaginary center line of the canoe and swept toward the bow. The paddler's arm positions do not change, only his or her waist

27

will twist. One or more strokes can be made on the opposite side of the craft before finishing with the forward sweep.

Figure 47. Setup cross draw sweep

Figure 48. Begin cross draw sweep

Figure 49. Finish with a forward sweep

The bow paddler is not changing paddling sides while performing the cross draw sweep; this stroke is merely an *extension* of the forward sweep's arc. Experienced paddlers use a feather during the period that the blade crosses over the bow breast plate.

Figure 50. Feathering across bow

Figure 51. Cross draw sweep - putting it all together

Now that we are experienced power stroke and forward sweep paddlers, we have some basic abilities to keep the canoe moving forward on a straight course. Gary and Lara will demonstrate.

Because Gary's stroke is more powerful than Lara's, the canoe's course tends to veer away from the side of his paddle. In this case,

Gary can compensate for this power differential by:
1. *Slowing* the rate at which he passes his blade through the water.
2. *Shortening* his blade's time in the water.
3. *Omitting* strokes as required.

Figure 52. Stronger paddler may slow blade speed through the water

Any of these three methods reduce the power of Gary's stroke to equal that of Lara's so that a straight paddling course is maintained.

Figure 53. Stronger paddler may omit strokes

30

Figure 54. Weaker paddler may add some forward sweep

If Lara wishes to make the corrective action for Gary's more powerful stroke, she can simply add some forward sweep to her stroke. This will reduce her forward power, but the straight course will be maintained because the bow is pushed back in line. Hence, Gary's more powerful stroke will not need to change.

Figure 55. Paddling straight makes for an enjoyable day

Crew Review

1. We discussed the importance of wearing a Type II or Type III PFD. (a) Describe the safety qualities of each type of PFD, and (2) give two or more examples of unexpected situations which would make you realize that wearing your PFD whenever you are boating is a pretty good idea.

2. (a) List three pieces of safety equipment discussed in the Crew Section and give a situation for each one's use. (b) Now name two items not discussed that could also be used as safety equipment - be creative.

3. Canoe nomenclature, or names of parts of the canoe, is a paddler's most important communication tool. Work from bow to stern listing as many parts of the canoe as you can.

4. Describe two ways of determining the correct paddle size so that when paddling on port, the distance between the left, or port hand, holding the neck, and the right, or starboard hand, holding the grip, feels comfortable for the paddler.

5. (a) Why do we step across the keel line as we "shift our weight" when boarding a canoe? (b) Describe the proper method for moving to one's seat.

6. The paddler leans out slightly and uses a hand-over-hand motion when performing the power stroke. (a) Which hand - the grip or control hand - makes the power stroke easier by pushing toward the bow? (b) Why do we want the blade to pass vertically through the water?

7. We can feel just how much easier feathering makes the out-of-water recovery portion of a stroke by holding the paddle with one hand in front of us and comparing the resistance between slicing the blade through the air versus pushing air with the blade faces. (a) When feathering during the forward power stroke, does the power face or reverse power face face the sky? (b) During the reverse power stroke?

8. In tandem paddling, the center of the canoe is generally the pivot point about which the canoe spins. (a) What does the term 'pivot point' really mean? (remember the revolving glass door analogy). (b) If the stern paddler weighs more than the bow paddler, which direction (fore or aft) will the 'pivot point' move?

9. Sweeps are most often used to make a stationary canoe spin about its pivot point. For best results, a good crew member knows to sweep the blade as far away from the pivot point as possible. Draw the top-view shape of a canoe and shade the regions where the bow paddler should make the 90° sweep arc. Now add the stern paddler's 90° arcs.

10. The cross draw sweep is merely an extension of the (forward / reverse) sweep?

Exercise:
Paddlers sometimes find their power strokes differ in power, causing the canoe to slowly change course. List corrective actions from the crew section the bow and stern paddlers can take to keep their canoe moving on a straight course. Prove these ideas by paddling with a partner on a straight course for ten canoe lengths, (paddle toward stationary objects, like trees), turn, and paddle ten canoe lengths back.

We're now one stroke along on our Paddle to Perfection!

Captain Tools

- nomenclature
- physical dimensions
- square knot
- sheet bend
- bowline

We will now add to the canoe nomenclature in our toolbox. The area inside the canoe is referred to as the **cockpit**. Inside the cockpit, we find the floor known as the **deck**, the curve on the sides called the **bilge**, some support pieces known as **ribs**, and the air pockets and flotation pieces at the bow and stern referred to as **floats**.

Figure 56. Top view of wooden canoe

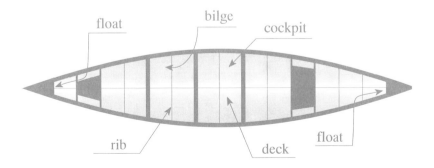

Figure 57. Additional canoe nomenclature

33

Besides knowing the names of the parts of the canoe, we should also know the names of some of its physical characteristics. The **length** of the canoe is the distance from the bow bang plate to the stern bang plate. The **beam** is the widest part of the canoe. The **draft** refers to the distance beneath the water's surface and the deepest point on the bottom of the canoe. And, the **freeboard** refers to the distance between the water's surface and the canoe's gunnel.

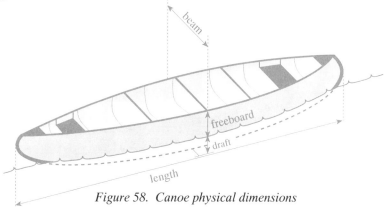

Figure 58. Canoe physical dimensions

Long canoes are generally fast and stable but slower to turn than short canoes. Wide canoes are generally more stable but slower than narrow canoes.

Good equipment makes for good canoeing. This paddle has been placed tip down in sand, causing chips and cracks. Placing the tip

Figure 59. Cracked tip caused by mishandling

on our shoe or standing the paddle on its grip will help to prevent this problem. Also, *canoes should be lifted into the water rather than slid* so as to keep them leak free and looking aesthetically pleasing.

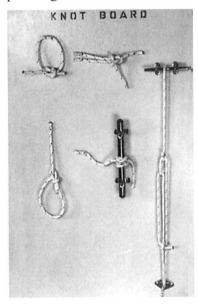

Paddlers often find the ability to tie knots useful during a day on the water. As good captains, we should be proficient in tying some simple knots. First, a piece of line has two ends: a **standing end**, which remains fixed, and a **running end**, which will be moving in our hands. Three knots often used in the sport of canoeing are the square knot, the sheet bend, and the bowline.

Figure 60. Paddler's knot board

Right over left then left over right makes the **square knot**. The square knot is useful for tying gear to the thwarts.

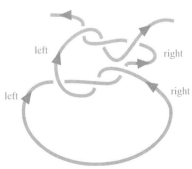

Figure 61. Square knot illustration

Figure 62. Square knot photo

If we want to tie two pieces of line together, we should use the square knot's cousin, the sheet bend. The **sheet bend** is tied like the square knot, but rather than bringing the running end through the loop, it goes back under itself.

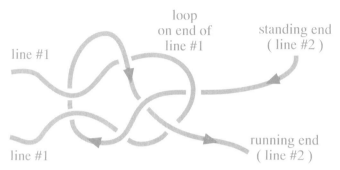

Figure 63. Sheet bend illustration

Figure 64. Sheet bend photograph

The **bowline** is used for making a temporary loop at the end of a line for uses such as a temporary dock line. To tie a bowline, one twists an overhand loop with the running end thumb and forefinger. Then, with the running end, "the rabbit comes out of the hole, goes around the tree, and jumps back into the hole."

Figure 65. Bowline illustration   *Figure 66. Bowline photograph*

Captain Practical

- launching the canoe
- capsizing
- canoe-over-canoe rescue
- Capistrano flip
- changing paddling positions

The **beam carry** portage is useful for short carries and launches. The canoe is floated onto the water using the **hand-over-hand pass**. Decide who will maintain contact with the canoe before it is fully on the water.

Figure 67. Beam carry portage　　*Figure 68. Maintain contact with canoe*

Two or more paddlers can use the **overhead carry** where narrow portaging paths make other portaging methods unusable. By tilting the canoe on the ground such that the cockpit faces away from us, gripping the thwarts and leaning back to position the canoe on our thighs, placing one hand on each gunnel, and hoisting the canoe to the overhead carry position, we can quickly achieve this portaging position. The overhead carry can be tiring and strenuous on the back, so use your best judgement when deciding to perform this carry.

Figure 69. Lift canoe onto thighs

Figure 70. Hold opposite side gunnel with outside hand

Figure 71. Lift canoe and balance overhead

Whenever we are afloat in a canoe, we have the potential to capsize. As captains of the craft, we should know how to safely handle a **capsizing**.

The best way to learn to remain calm during a capsize event is to practice one in a controlled **capsizing drill**. The controlled capsizing drill is usually performed in the following manner. First, paddles are stowed on the deck. Second, paddlers move to the center of the craft, one at a time, and sit on the deck with their legs over the same gunnel. Third, with their midship-side hands, the paddlers hold onto the gunnel behind them to be certain the gunnel will not strike them on their heads.

Figure 72. Safe capsizing drill method

Figure 73. Count heads

Allowing the canoe to slowly fill with water over the side rather than causing it to flip is a safe technique to control a canoe capsize. During the controlled capsizing drill, we should follow the **self-rescue procedure**. As good captains, we and our crew stay with the craft except in an emergency because a lone swimmer is much more difficult to spot than a canoe.

The three steps performed after any capsize event are: one, save yourself; two, count heads to be sure everyone is safe; three, call for help using your audible and/or visual distress signals.

If no help is available, we can rescue ourselves by using the **swamped-canoe swim**. Slide into the canoe, one at a time, and sit on the deck. Next, enjoy a leisurely hand paddle to shore.

Figure 74. Re-entering swamped canoe

Figure 75. Self-rescue - hand paddle

41

If an assisting canoe is available, use the **canoe-over-canoe rescue** procedure:

1. The canoes are put into the **beam-to-end rescue position**.

Figure 76. Rescue canoe approaches swamped canoe

Figure 77. Beam-to-end rescue position

2. Members of both teams go to the **canoe-over-canoe rescue positions** (rescue paddlers at midship and one capsized paddler straddling the rescue canoe while the other helps position the capsized canoe).

3. The capsized canoe is **turtled** (rolled such that the cockpit faces the water to allow water to drain when hoisted onto the rescue canoe's gunnels), and both capsized paddlers straddle the rescue canoe.

4. The rescuers now break the turtled canoe's water seal to enable hoisting and suspending the capsized canoe on the gunnels of the rescue canoe.

Figure 78. Paddlers prepare for canoe-over-canoe rescue

Figure 79. Rotate canoe to break water seal

5. The rescue paddlers balance the capsized canoe on the rescue canoe's gunnels to drain.
6. The rescuers roll the drained canoe on the rescue canoe's gunnels.
7. The rescue paddlers use the beam carry method to place the emptied canoe back onto the water.
8. The rescue paddlers bring the canoes side-by-side and hold.
9. The rescuers support the emptied canoe while one capsized canoe member at a time re-enters the emptied canoe.
10. Gear is now collected.

note: The capsized paddlers' physical condition should be checked before and after rescue, paying special attention for signs of hypothermia and shock. Immediately seek medical care if treatment is necessary.

Figure 80. Canoe-over-canoe rescue illustration

The last capsize rescue is a self-rescue called the **Capistrano flip**. Paddlers go under the turtled canoe, break the water seal, kick three times, and toss the canoe. *The Capistrano flip is a difficult maneuver, so be prepared with alternate methods of rescue.*

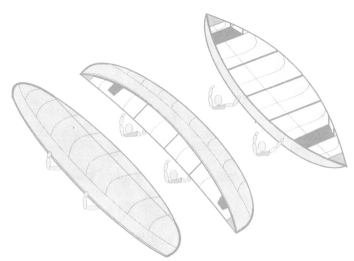

Figure 81. Capistrano flip

A good captain should be both a proficient bow and stern paddler. This means that paddlers should change positions while afloat so no skill goes unrehearsed. We use what is known as the **leapfrog method** for changing places within the canoe.

First, Lara and Mark stow their paddles. Next, Lara, the bow paddler, moves to the center of the craft and gets low. Now, Mark, the stern paddler, crosses over Lara while moving to the bow. Lara

Figure 82. Stow paddles

Figure 83. Bow paddler moves first

and Mark hold the gunnels whenever moving in the canoe to maintain balance and to keep the center of gravity in the canoe low. After the change of positions is complete, Lara and Mark pick-up their paddles, and they are underway.

Figure 84. Stern paddler 'leapfrogs' over bow paddler

Figure 85. Paddlers are underway

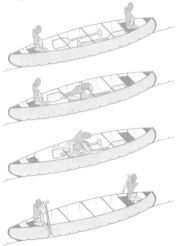

Figure 86. Leapfrog illustration

Captain Strokes

- **J-stroke**
- **moveable strokes**
- **stationary strokes**
- **sideslipping and pivoting**
- **high and low braces**
- **tandem Duffek stroke**
- **coordinating strokes**

The stern paddler paddling on starboard or port can head the canoe more starboard or port, respectively, by using the J-stroke. The **J-stroke** begins exactly like the forward power stroke, but after the blade passes the paddler's side, the power face is rotated outward and the blade is pushed away from the canoe until the stroke is complete. The blade carves a 'J' or backward-'J' in the water; hence, the J-stroke.

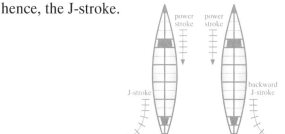

Figure 87. J-stroke top view

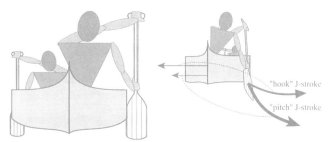

Figure 88. Stern paddler overpowers bow paddler

Figure 89. Stern paddler applies J-stroke compensation

A J-stroke can be performed to varying degrees. The **pitch-J** adds only a slight pushaway; the pitch-J is used for slight course adjustments. The **hook-J** refers to the case when the blade is forced almost directly outward upon reaching the paddler's side. The hook-J is used for large course adjustments and tends to drastically reduce the canoe's forward momentum.

Figure 90. Pitch-J stroke

Figure 91. Hook-J stroke

There are times when we want to move a stationary canoe directly sideways. To do this, we have the moveable draw, the moveable pry, and the pushaway strokes. The moveable draw is used to move the canoe sideways toward the paddle, or *draw* it toward the paddle. The moveable pry and pushaway are used to move the canoe sideways away from the paddle, or *pry or push* it away from the paddle. To set-up these strokes, turn the blade into position by raising back the control hand wrist.

The **moveable draw** begins with the paddle extended to the side of the paddler away from the canoe. The **pushaway stroke** begins with the blade to the immediate side of the paddler.

Figure 92. Starting pushaway

48

Figure 93. Finishing pushaway

Raising back the control hand wrist causes the power face to face the paddler during the moveable draw and pushaway strokes. Also, a blade provides more sideward force when moving water toward or away from the canoe rather than forcing water up or down.

Two recovery methods for the moveable draw and moveable pry are the out-of-water recovery and the in-the-water recovery. The paddler using the **out-of-water recovery** gets the blade back to the starting position by raising the blade completely out of the water between each moveable stroke.

The paddler using the **in-the-water recovery** gets the blade back to the starting position by rotating the blade sideways between each moveable stroke such that the power face faces the stern. The in-the-water recovery is more efficient than the out-of-water recovery, but takes some practice to master.

One may find the pushaway to be physically difficult due to the body mechanics used to perform this stroke, so we have another pushaway stroke, the **moveable pry**. Hook the control-hand thumb under the gunnel, lay the

Figure 94. In-the-water recovery

control-hand fingers over the shaft to provide the pivot point, and pry. An in-the-water recovery is performed by turning the grip-hand thumb outward.

Figure 95. Beginning moveable pry

Figure 96. Finishing moveable pry

Figure 97. In-the-water recovery

For the overachievers who do not want to lose any time with a recovery, we also have the sculling draw and sculling pushaway. Their basic action can be compared to spreading peanut butter on soft bread.

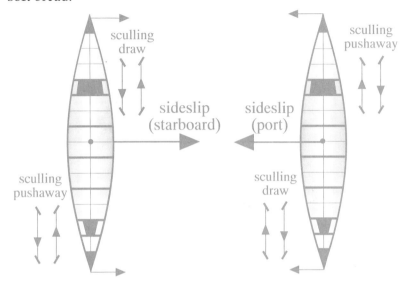

Figure 98. Sculling strokes

While sculling the blade back and forth during the **sculling draw**, we keep the blade held vertical in the water and maintain a blade angle of about 30° with the leading edge away from the canoe. For the **sculling pushaway**, the leading edge is toward the canoe. *The longer the stroke, the more power each pass will produce.*

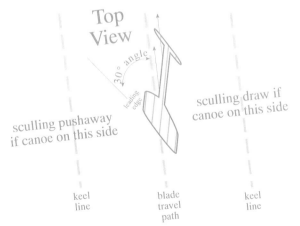

Figure 99. Sculling stroke blade positions

Let's put these moveable strokes together. If each paddler performs the same moveable stroke, the canoe will spin. If one

Figure 100. Spinning starboard using moveable strokes

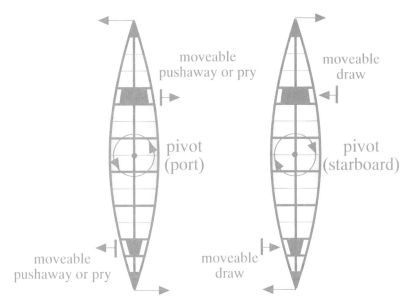

Figure 101. Spinning using moveable strokes

paddler performs a moveable draw while the other performs a pushaway, the canoe travels sideways. The stern paddler is responsible for calling out signals telling the bow paddler how to adjust the power of his or her stroke to keep the canoe moving directly sideways. Good captain paddlers should be versed in the moveable stroke combinations and their effects on the canoe.

Figure 102. Sideslipping to starboard using moveable strokes

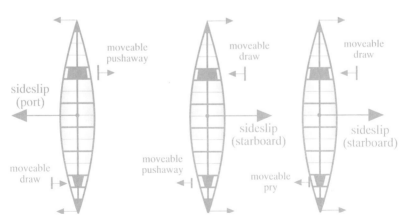

Figure 103. Sideslipping using moveable strokes

We now know how to make a stationary canoe turn and move sideways, but often we may want to perform these actions on a canoe which has *forward momentum*. The special strokes we use to make a *moving* canoe pivot and sideslip are called stationary strokes, namely the stationary draw, the stationary pry, and the stationary cross draw. (We will later use these strokes to form our river stroke combinations while running the river.)

Figure 104. Sideslipping using stationary strokes

The difference between the moveable strokes and the stationary strokes is that the moveable strokes require paddler power, whereas the stationary strokes use only the power of the canoe's movement.

Because the bow paddler has an unobstructed view of the water immediately in front of the canoe, the bow paddler will call sideslip or pivot and each paddler will perform the appropriate stationary stroke. A typical command call is, "pivot right!" Another command call is "sideslip right!"

Figure 105. Bow calls stroke command

54

Let's take a detailed look at the blade positions during the stationary strokes. We'll start with the **stationary draw**. The blade is held perpendicular to the surface of the water with the leading edge angled *outward* at approximately 30°. The control-hand wrist is raised back to support the blade, whose power face will be taking the force of the water.

Paddlers should raise their grip arm only as high as the forehead to reduce shoulder injury risk.

Figure 106. Stationary stroke paddling positions

The **stationary pry** blade position is again with the blade held perpendicular to the water's surface but with the leading edge angled 30° *toward* the canoe. The reverse face will be struck by the rushing water. To get the blade into position, slice the blade through the water at the 30° angle until it bumps the canoe. Since the blade has greater effect during a stationary stroke when farther away from the canoe's pivot point (the center of the canoe), Mark, the bow paddler, places his blade as far forward as is comfortable, while Gary in the stern places his blade behind him.

Let's now understand the effect of the **stationary stroke combinations** on the canoe. The *same* stationary stroke combinations, draw-draw or pry-pry, will cause the canoe to *spin* about the pivot point. The *opposite* stroke combinations, draw-pry or pry-draw, will cause the canoe to *sideslip*. The imaginary line extending out from the blade's leading edge indicates the direction in which that end of the canoe will be steered.

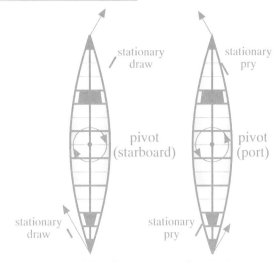

Figure 107. Stationary stroke pivoting

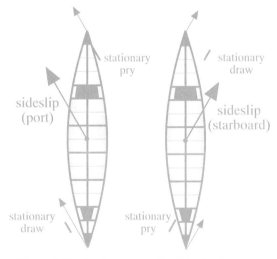

Figure 108. Stationary stroke sideslipping

To practice the stationary stroke combinations, the paddlers should count three good strokes and then apply the stationary stroke combination to ... **pivot port** ... **pivot starboard** ... **sideslip port** ... **sideslip starboard**. As good captains, we should switch paddling positions to get comfortable with both bow and stern strokes.

The last stationary stroke we will be learning is called the **stationary cross draw**. The bow paddler can use a stationary cross draw to achieve the same result as the stationary pry. To apply, simply hold the initial cross draw sweep position.

Figure 109. Pivot using stationary cross draw

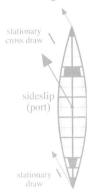

Figure 110. Sideslipping using stationary cross draw

When applying *any* stationary stroke, the paddler should be prepared to adjust the blade angle; too much angle will cause the craft to stop, and too little angle will not yield the desired results. *Practice is the best method for really learning how to angle the blade most effectively.*

Figure 111. Adjust blade angle

next two strokes, the high brace and low brace, are used to rebalance a leaning canoe. The **high brace** is performed by placing the *power face* on the water and applying pressure with the control hand. While pushing up with the grip hand, we slide the canoe toward our blade using our hips. We keep our grip hand arm low and in front of us to avoid shoulder injury.

Figure 112. High brace

The **low brace** is performed by placing the *reverse face* flat on the water. Paddlers use the low brace as a quick response to right a leaning canoe.

Figure 113. Low brace

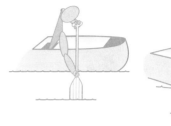

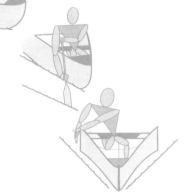

The Duffek stroke is the last stroke we will be learning in the captain section. The **Duffek stroke** combines four strokes we have already learned: the stationary draw, high brace, moveable draw toward bow, and forward power stroke. The Duffek stroke is an *active* stroke that provides the bow paddler with a powerful method for turning the bow toward the blade while maintaining headway.

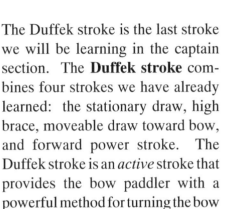

Figure 114. Duffek stroke

Figure 115. Tandem Duffek stroke start

The Duffek by the bow paddler, combined with the stationary draw into a sweeping power stroke by the stern paddler, can get a canoe to spin on a dime with momentum into the new paddling course. An experienced paddler combines the stationary draw...

high brace...moveable draw toward bow...and forward power stroke into one fluid motion.

Figure 116. Tandem Duffek stroke finish

Now that we have covered all of our flat water tandem canoeing strokes, we should practice coordinating paddling to reduce the energy each paddler exerts. Note that the stern paddler is responsible for maintaining stroke coordination since the stern paddler can see the bow paddler's blade. By **paddling synchronously**, neither paddler tries to pull the entire weight of the canoe alone.

Figure 117. Tandem paddling teamwork

The stern paddler should also be prepared to change paddling sides and lay in stationary strokes as called out by the bow paddler. In all circumstances, however, *both paddlers must communicate to maintain good tandem paddling teamwork.*

Captain Review

1. (a) List the canoe nomenclature we learned in the Captain section. (b) List some canoe physical dimensions.

2. What is one use for the square knot? The sheet bend? The bowline? Tie each.

3. Starting with the paddlers sitting on the seats, (a) list (in order) the steps for safely inducing a capsize, as described in the Captain Practical section. (b) How can paddlers rescue themselves if no assisting craft is available? (c) List (in order) a canoe-over-canoe rescue.

4. (a) Why do bow and stern paddlers change places every so often? (b) The center of gravity in the canoe is kept _____ by using the leapfrog method for changing places.

5. (a) The _____ paddler uses the J-stroke to make a paddling course correction rather than the bow paddler's performing a forward sweep because the J-stroke tends to be a more efficient method. (b) The (pitch / hook) J-stroke is used for making slight course adjustments; (c) the (pitch / hook) J-stroke is used for making large course adjustments.

6. Draw the top-view of a canoe. (a) If the bow paddler does a moveable draw on port, what moveable stroke(s) can the stern paddler perform to sideslip the stationary canoe to port? (b) Spin the stationary canoe to port? (adding lines to represent paddles and arrows to indicate paddle movement may help). Now the bow paddler performs a moveable pry on starboard. The stern paddler can (c) use a moveable (draw / pushaway) to spin the canoe to port and (d) use a moveable (draw / pushaway) to sideslip the canoe to port.

7. Draw the top-view of a canoe. (a) If the bow paddler places a stationary draw on port, what stationary stroke can the stern paddler perform to sideslip the moving canoe to port? (b) Pivot the moving canoe to port? Now the bow paddler performs a stationary pry on starboard. The stern paddler can (c) use a stationary (draw / pry) to pivot the canoe to port and (d) use a stationary (draw / pry) to sideslip the canoe to port.

8. (a) The stationary cross draw is like which other stationary stroke? (b) Which paddler can use the stationary cross draw? (c) Relative to the keel line, approximately what blade angle is held by all stationary strokes?

9. Either a high brace or low brace can be used to right a leaning canoe. (a) The power face pushes on the water during the (high / low) brace? (b) The reverse face pushes on the water during the (high / low) brace? (c) Why does the paddler hold him or herself to the canoe securely with his or her legs when performing either of these brace strokes?

10. The Duffek stroke is an active stroke that provides the bow paddler with a powerful method for turning the bow toward the blade while maintaining headway. What four strokes are combined to form the Duffek stroke?

Exercise:
Set up a floating obstacle course (using buoys, rafts, or moored boats). With a captain paddling partner, run this course several times. Be sure to vary the direction travelled around obstacles and bow and stern paddling places in the canoe. Try to reduce the time each pass takes through the course.

We're now one more stroke along on our Paddle to Perfection!

Solo Tools

- canoe materials
- rolling hitch

Some common open **canoe construction materials** are wood, aluminum, plastic, fiberglass, ABS, and Kevlar. The material from which a canoe is made contributes to the canoe's attributes, such as: durability, ease of repair, weight, quietness in water, aesthetics, and cost. We should determine our paddling needs before choosing a canoe type.

The **rolling hitch** is useful for securing a canoe to a pole because the rolling hitch will not slip. The rolling hitch is performed by making two turns around the pole with the running end - overlapping the standing end on each turn - and completed by making an underhand loop around the pole above the standing end.

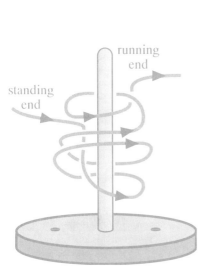

Figure 118. Rolling hitch illustration   Figure 119. Rolling hitch photograph

Solo Paddling Practical

- portaging
- seating locations
- wind effects

As solo paddlers, we often find ourselves in the position of portaging the canoe alone, so it is a good idea to be prepared by knowing safe **solo portaging** methods.

Figure 120. Solo portaging - leg walk

A solo paddler can bring the canoe up to his or her thighs and perform the **leg walk**. Gary tilts the cockpit away from himself, holds the midship thwart or **yoke** (a curved thwart, located at midship in many solo canoes, that is designed for a paddler to rest the canoe on his or her shoulders comfortably during a shoulder carry portage), and hoists the canoe up to his thighs using his weight. Keeping one's back straight when walking the canoe to the water will reduce back injury risk. The leg walk is suitable for short distance carries.

Clever solo paddlers team up and use the **two-person two-canoe breastplate carry**. The canoes naturally balance and walking is unimpaired. The two-person two-canoe breastplate carry facilitates long distance portaging.

Figure 121. Two-person two-canoe carry

Many paddlers consider solo paddling a very relaxing and elegant form of canoeing. Having completed the Crew and Captain sections, we could conceivably solo paddle a canoe at this point, but let's learn a little more about this subject before we try.

A question many students ask when first introduced to solo paddling is, "Where should I sit?" This is a good question, but it would be better worded, "Where should the pivot point be located when solo canoeing?" The answer is, "It depends on wind and water current conditions." The canoe is like a **weathervane** when exposed to wind and water currents; the pivot point, generally located beneath the paddler, acts as the weathervane pedestal. The end of the canoe closer to the pivot point will tend to point into the wind and water currents.

Figure 122. Mark and duck discussing solo seating locations

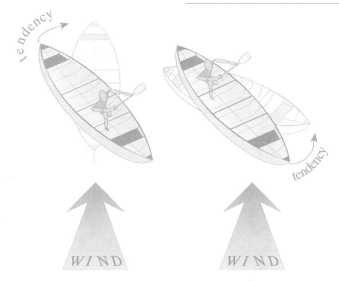

Figure 123. Weathervane analogy

This weathervane analogy means when paddling into the wind, the solo paddler should move toward the bow. When paddling away from the wind, the solo paddler should move toward the stern. When paddling across the wind, the solo paddler should kneel in the middle of the canoe. *Adjusting the weight on the canoe helps keep the canoe pointed in the desired direction, thereby keeping the solo paddler's effort low.*

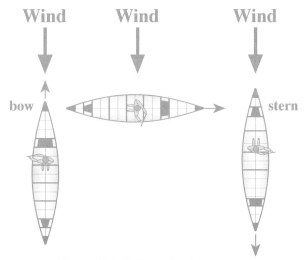

Figure 124. Solo seating locations

An experienced solo paddler is able to travel long distances in a straight line. When wind is present, a skilled solo paddler will make the necessary seating adjustments to eliminate the need for using correction strokes. **Correction strokes** mean that not all of the paddler's stroke goes into propelling the canoe forward, so the paddler will, in essence, be saving energy by positioning him or herself properly relative to the wind. Be patient because this sense of hull balance will take some practice to develop.

Figure 125. Solo seating position relative to wind

Solo Strokes

- **C-stroke**
- **pivot turns**
- **moveable strokes**
- **solo Duffek Stroke**

The solo paddler is faced with the challenge of controlling the canoe without the assistance of a partner. As good solo paddlers, we would like to avoid switching paddling sides very often because it makes for an inefficient and tired paddler. In fact, because experienced solo paddlers paddle on the side opposite the wind to balance power strokes, we realize that the solo paddler may not wish to switch paddling sides for many minutes at a time. This does not necessarily mean that the solo paddler's stroke be strong, it need only be efficient.

Figure 126. Gary, Mark, and Lara discuss solo paddling

In the Solo Strokes section, we will expand upon the strokes we learned as tandem paddlers to make solo paddling an equally exciting experience.

During startup, beginner solo paddlers find the canoe rotates away from the paddle and must be corrected by a hook-J. To offset the rotation, experienced solo paddlers add a small arc toward the canoe at the beginning of the power stroke and finish with a hook- or pitch-J - this is known as the **C-stroke**. Once underway, the power stroke can be used with just a pitch-J.

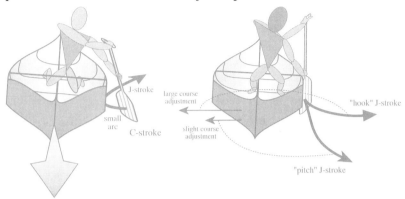

Figure 127. Solo C-stroke   Figure 128. Solo J-stroke

Tandem paddlers sweep the blade in a 90° arc as far away from the canoe's pivot point as possible for maximized mechanical advantage over the canoe. Because the solo paddler is seated directly above the canoe's pivot point, he or she *can and should* sweep a full 180° arc for maximum spin power.

The solo paddler wishing to pivot the canoe has two choices: an outside pivot turn or an inside pivot turn - outside and inside refer to the side of the canoe the paddle is stroking relative to the turning direction.

The **outside pivot turn** is simply the forward sweeps with which

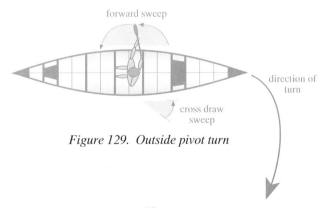

Figure 129. Outside pivot turn

68

Figure 130. Outside pivot turns

we are now very comfortable. Adding the cross draw sweep can add that little extra *umph* to the turn.

The **inside pivot turn** for solo paddling is a combination of a reverse sweep and a sweeping draw stroke. When the blade reaches the paddler's side, the paddler rotates his or her control wrist up and back to perform the sweeping draw stroke portion of the inside-pivot stroke. A natural in-the-water recovery is used to get the blade into position for the next stroke.

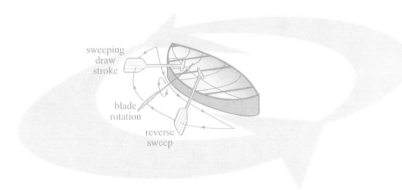

Figure 131. Inside pivot turn

Solo paddlers often prefer the sculling version of the moveable draw and pushaway strokes because of their efficiency and because the sculling strokes are quite graceful, matching the image the solo paddler often wishes to project.

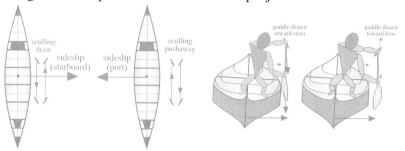

Figure 132. Solo sculling strokes - sideslipping

Figure 133. Solo sculling draw

The solo paddler can navigate a 90° turn using a Duffek stroke. The paddler paddles into the turn and lays in the Duffek stroke (stationary draw, high brace, moveable draw toward bow, and forward power stroke). Like all solo paddling strokes, the Duffek stroke should look seamless and effortless.

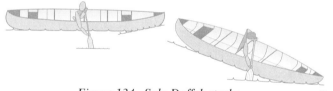

Figure 134. Solo Duffek stroke

Figure 135. Solo paddle in pairs

Solo Review

1. Canoes are made of many types of materials, such as: wood, aluminum, fiberglass, ABS, and Kevlar. The materials contribute to a canoe's durability. What other attributes are affected by the material from which the canoe is made?

2. The rolling hitch is a useful knot for tying a floating canoe to a pole because the rolling hitch will not _____. Tie a rolling hitch.

3. (a) The solo paddler often uses the leg walk portage for (short / long) distance carries. (b) Clever solo paddlers team up and use which portaging technique?

4. Given that the paddler basically controls the location of the canoe's pivot point and the end of the canoe closer to the canoe's pivot point will tend to point into the wind and/or water current (recall the weathervane analogy). Toward which end of the canoe would a good solo paddler sit when paddling directly into a strong headwind?

5. Solo paddlers save energy by using a power stroke without a pitch J-stroke when paddling a straight course so that all of the blade's power goes into propelling the canoe forward. When paddling across the wind, the solo paddler paddles on the canoe side opposite the wind, or leeward side (as opposed to windward side). (a) How will the wind balance off a power stroke? (b) How can the solo paddler use his or her position in the canoe to balance off the power stroke so as to reduce need for the J-stroke?

6. Solo paddlers use the C-stroke at startup. (a) Why? (b) What strokes appear to be combined to form the C-stroke?

7. The solo paddler can perform an efficient outside pivot turn by sweeping the blade in a full 180° arc whereas tandem paddlers' sweeps are only efficient in a 90° arc. What is the cause of this difference?

8. The inside pivot stroke refers to spinning the canoe toward the paddling side (i.e., the paddle is on the inside of the turn). (a) What two strokes are combined to make an inside pivot stroke? (b) How do we get the blade back to starting position?

9. Gracefulness is a quality a solo paddler may often wish to project so they may choose to use the _____ version of the moveable draw to make a stationary canoe move sideways.

10. The Duffek stroke is aided by leaning (into / away from) the turn?

Exercise:
Navigate through the same floating obstacle course. Does using only inside pivot turns reduce the time through the course compared to using only outside pivot turns? Compare using only outside pivot turns to using only the Duffek stroke. Try paddling this course without changing paddling sides.

We're now one stroke from completing our Paddle to Perfection!

River Team Tools

- river gear
- artificial respiration

Running a river can be a thrilling experience, but a river is no place to canoe without the proper safety equipment. This means that we should have the equipment recommended for flat water paddling on hand.

We also recommend **safety equipment** specific to river paddling, including: a **bag-type heaving line** (containing soft thick line), **flotation** to add buoyancy to the canoe, and **duct tape** for making quick temporary repairs to the canoe.

Figure 136. Bag-type heaving line

Figure 137. Flotation

Figure 138. Duct tape

72

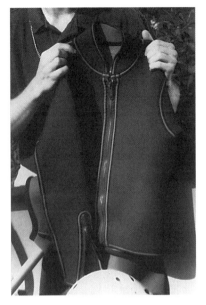

In addition to river canoeing safety equipment, paddlers should also be prepared with appropriate **river clothing**. *The basic rule-of-thumb for the mandatory wearing of either a **wetsuit** or **drysuit** is when the*

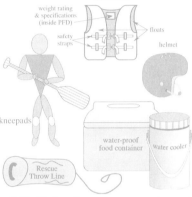

Figure 139. Appropriate river clothing

Figure 140. Take all necessary equipment

air and water temperatures do not add up to be greater than 100° Fahrenheit, which is 38° Celsius. Our PFD's should protect our entire upper bodies, including the back, and should be comfortable for long periods of paddling.

Depending on the strength of the river and our familiarity with the river, we may wish to include a **helmet** as a piece of our standard

Figure 141. Wear appropriate headwear and footwear

white water river gear. Of course, we always wear proper footwear while river paddling.

River paddling requires plenty of energy, so packing food in **waterproof containers** is a good idea. A hot or cold drink may also be appreciated. Remember to tie all this gear securely to the canoe if taking it along. We should accept the potential for an unexpected capsize and be prepared accordingly.

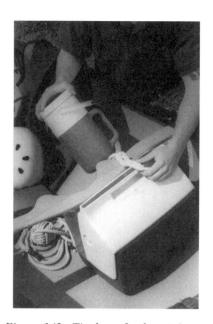

Figure 142. Tie down food containers

Figure 143. Lara discusses artificial respiration

Artificial respiration knowledge lends itself well to canoeing because of the potential danger associated with the sport. As always, be prepared by knowing Red Cross standards, learning current medical artificial respiration techniques, and using common sense.

River Team Practical

- selecting the river
- transporting the canoe
- diver's hitch
- taut line hitch
- fisherman's knot
- reading the river
- scouting the river
- river obstructions
- swimming the river
- river capsizing

Selection of the right river should be based on paddlers' skill and experience as *river* paddlers. **Rivers are classified** from one to six for canoes, where class 6 is considered most difficult. We suggest rivers of class one or two after developing proficient canoe handling skills. Be aware that rivers tend to flow much faster in times of **runoff**, as in springtime. *Call ahead for seasonal information about rivers you may wish to explore.*

Figure 144. Selecting the river

After selecting the river, we may need to **transport a canoe** to the river, so a river team should know how to secure a canoe to the roof of a car. We begin by centering the canoe on a sturdy set of **roof racks**. With some strong line, such as 1/2" nylon or dacron, the canoe's bow and stern are tied directly to the car frame.

The hull should be secured in place using some **bungee cord** or straps specially designed for the car rack system. We may also wish to tie the thwarts to the rack using several wraps of line and an appropriate hitch or knot. *Be overcautious - nothing is worse than seeing your canoe follow you down the interstate highway.*

Figure 145. Center canoe on racks

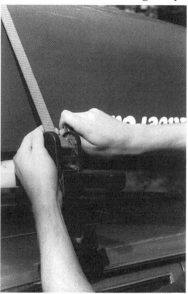

Figure 146. Strap canoe to racks

Two knots used in canoe transport are the diver's hitch and the taut line hitch. To tie the **diver's hitch**, twist the line two times, bring a loop through the loop at the end of the twist, and tighten.

To tie the **taut line hitch**, we turn the running end around the taut line and between the standing end two times, then finish with an overhand loop below the standing end. The taut line hitch is secured by sliding the hitch along the taut line in the direction of the running end until it holds tight.

This configuration works great

Figure 147. Transport knot combination

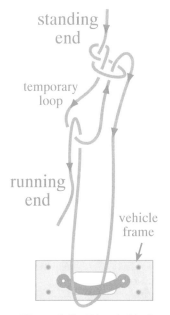

Figure 148. Diver's hitch

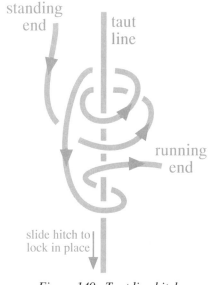

Figure 149. Taut line hitch

for locking down a canoe because the diver's hitch increases our pulling force, and the taut line hitch locks the line in place.

A **fisherman's knot** can be used to secure the line to the frame of the car.

Figure 150. Fisherman's knot

Figure 151. Secure canoe to roof rack

As river team paddlers, we must know how to **read the river** to avoid damaging the canoe and to ensure our safety.

"Reading the river" is another way of saying, "determining the safest navigational passageway through potential hazards found on the river." This passageway, usually the highest body of flowing water, can generally be found in midstream in a straight channel and toward the outer edge around a bend.

Figure 152. Scouting the river

Scouting a river before running it is invaluable for locating the best passageway. Scouting a river means to physically visit a

Figure 153. Scouting river for hidden obstructions

section of river, paying particular attention to **river obstructions**, such as: rocks, logs, branches, shallow water, and unmanageable water.

"Paddle to Perfection!"
River Scouting Report
Androscoggin River, Errol, NH

1. Calm water just below dam. Water moving slowly - can see class 2 water begin to move around bend.
2. Class 1 & 2. Rocks, white water. Nice trees on other side. Small paths to water from campground.
3. Class 2 & 3. Can see class 2 upstream. Can see class 3 upstream and downstream. Above and below water river obstructions and eddy are here.
4. Class 3 standing waves and eddies near river bank.
5. Class 2 & 3 standing waves. Rough water ferrying location.
6. Slow moving water. Flat. Nice reflections of pines across river.
7. Class 1 to 2 water transition. Excellent location for ferrying drill. Canoe transport practice location.
8. Fast moving class 2 & 3. Good location for sideslipping drills. Class 3 filled with below water river obstructions. Stay left. Strainer in middle.
9. Overlook. Lunch stop. Class 2 water below.
10. Stationary to class 1 water. Before Brown Co. Bridge.
11. Brown Co. Bridge overlooking standing waves. River rider & capsizing drill. Safe, open-end, upstream 'V'.
12. Big, safe, standing waves.
note: map for reference purposes only (river conditions subject to change)

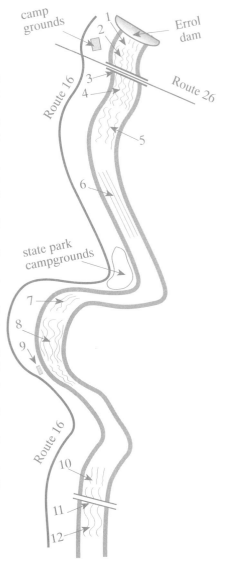

Figure 154. Detailed river map

Having a detailed **river map** will prove useful in the scouting process. We recommend speaking with experienced paddlers about the visible and hidden obstructions in the river.

River obstructions can be identified by a paddler on the water through understanding the way water flows when making contact with river obstructions.

Flowing water tends to climb up objects that break the surface of the water - paddlers label this water formation a **cushion**. Experienced river team paddlers recognize an object just below the water's surface by the calm dark spot surrounded by flowing water - the calm spot over the rock is referred to as a **pillow**.

Figure 155. Cushion and pillow

A **hole**, or water which flows back on itself, indicates a very large rock is beneath the water's surface immediately upstream of this hole; paddlers do well to stay clear of these because a hole tends to hold the canoe, often resulting in a capsize.

Figure 156. Hole

Horizon lines across a river are either **low head dams** or **waterfalls**. River team paddlers should portage around these river formations because of sharp dropoffs and risk of striking debris that may be trapped in or about these water formations. **Strainers**

are large branches, above or below the water's surface, usually found in the river near the river banks. Strainers hardly alter river flow and should be avoided at all cost. A river paddler getting caught in a strainer will be forced underwater by the river current; this is often fatal. Lines separating rough water and calm water are **eddy lines**, where the smooth water area sheltered behind the above-water river obstruction is referred to as an **eddy**.

Figure 157. Eddy line and eddy

Standing waves are caused by heavy water flow over objects that are generally located a safe distance beneath the water's surface.

Figure 158. V - open end downstream

A 'V' with its **open end downstream** lets us know an object to be avoided is at the 'V's point, closest to us when approaching this water formation.

A 'V' with its **open end upstream** is a sign that water is being forced between two objects. This rough, fast water flowing through the objects is called a **chute**. Paddlers should steer through chutes like these and enjoy the ride!

Figure 159. V - open end upstream

Now let's discuss the safety responsibilities of a paddler who finds him or herself in the river. First, *do not panic. If you relax, you may actually enjoy the ride.* Next, get into the **river rider position**, which is on one's back with feet leading downstream and up at the water's surface. This position prepares us to fend off obstructions and ensures our legs stay clear of riverbed rocks; *getting feet or legs trapped beneath river bed rocks will hold the river rider beneath the water's surface and can be fatal.*

Figure 160. River rider position

If the river rider must go it alone, he or she should stay in river rider position, use the river's power by angling 30° toward the river bank, and perform a hand paddle to shore. The river rider should be checked for signs of hypothermia and shock once safely ashore.

Figure 161. Throw bag toss

Figure 162. Throw bag rescue

The river rider should make an attempt to stay with and upstream of the canoe whenever possible; a canoe is much less likely to be forced underwater than a lone swimmer. Staying with the canoe will also make receiving help and reaching the river bank easier.

A difficult situation is, of course, a **river capsizing**. Follow the rules we just covered: get feet to the water's surface and pointed downstream, get to the upstream end of the canoe, roll the canoe cockpit face up, angle the upstream end of the canoe 30° toward the river bank, use the river current to help in swimming the canoe to the river bank, and check paddlers' physical conditions once ashore. Above all else, *remain calm and wait until reaching the river bank before attempting to stand.* We should note that a swamped canoe can

Figure 163. Stay with canoe

have the effective weight of more than a thousand pounds (over four hundred fifty kilograms) in moving water, which is why staying upstream of the canoe is highly encouraged.

Although we will always paddle with others, we must be sure that we are properly prepared for our day on the river. Paddling in the accompaniment of an experienced scout is always a wise idea. Finally, *never underestimate the power of moving water.*

Figure 164. River capsizing

River Team Strokes

- ferrying
- eddy turns
- peel outs
- shooting the rapids
- running the river

In the River Team Strokes section, we will be demonstrating the **combination stroke skills** used to control the canoe while running the river. We will find our flat water sideslipping and pivoting practice during the Captain Strokes section valuable in navigating the white water.

Let's begin with a relatively simple drill known as ferrying. **Ferrying** is used to traverse back and forth across the river. Like any new skill, we first practice in a section of river that we can handle to build some confidence.

While ferrying, river team paddlers angle their canoe's bow between 0 and 30 degrees toward the river bank they wish to reach. River team paddlers should practice ferrying across the river in both directions and facing downstream. River team paddlers should learn to use the moving water more than paddler power to traverse across the current before continuing downstream to more active sections of river. Also, river team paddlers should spend some time learning how to communicate on the river with simple "right!" and "left!" commands.

Figure 165. Ferrying practice

Once confident with the ferrying skill, paddlers should welcome the challenge of playing in rougher water. *In faster flowing water, leaning downstream becomes important to prevent the water rushing under the canoe from rolling the canoe to the upstream side.* Kneeling in the canoe to lower the center of gravity makes the canoe more stable, which is necessary when river paddling.

An important skill with which river team paddlers should familiarize themselves is the eddy turn. An **eddy turn** provides paddlers with a method of getting their canoe behind a river current obstruction, such as a large above-water rock, to allow for some rest and/or scouting of the next section of river.

Figure 166. Beginning an eddy turn

Figure 167. Completing an eddy turn

Figure 168. Another eddy turn

River teams use two basic combinations of strokes when making eddy turns. The first combination is the case of making an eddy turn to the bow paddler's paddling side. The bow paddler uses the tandem Duffek in conjunction with the stern paddler's stationary draw and forward sweeps. The high brace of the Duffek stroke is timed to be placed in the calm eddy water after paddling strongly across the eddy line at an angle between 30 and 45 degrees. By placing the high brace in the calm eddy water, the paddle blade

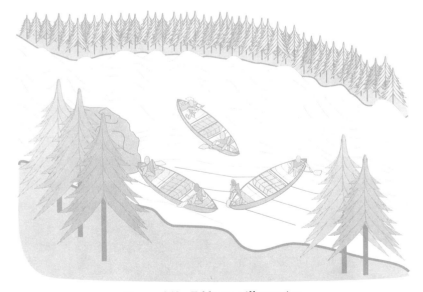

Figure 169. Eddy turn illustration

acts like a post about which the canoe will revolve. River team paddlers lean into the turn once in the eddy, *as if riding a bicycle.* The high brace of the Duffek provides the righting force necessary to prevent a capsize. We should note that the stern paddler, using power strokes after the combination of stationary draw and forward sweeps, does not attempt to paddle the stern into the eddy *until* more than one-half of the canoe has crossed into the eddy. Attempting to get the stern into the eddy too soon can result in the bow being turned back into the moving water.

The second eddy turn stroke combination is the case of turning to the side opposite the bow paddler's paddling side. The bow paddler uses the stationary cross draw in conjunction with the stern paddler's reverse sweep into a low brace. We should be aware that, during the stationary cross draw, the blade is placed in the eddy water *after* the bow has crossed the eddy line at an angle between 30 and 45 degrees. Again, the paddlers lean into the turn once in the eddy, as if riding a bicycle. The righting force in this case is the low brace performed by the stern paddler. One question which may arise is, "Could the stationary pry have been used rather than the stationary cross draw while turning the canoe into the eddy?" The answer is that a stationary pry tends to make the paddle act like a lever that may potentially capsize the canoe to the downstream side, so we are better off using the stationary cross draw, which also helps us lean into the turn.

Figure 170. Stationary cross draw and reverse sweep

Figure 171. Stationary cross draw and low brace

Figure 172. Completed opposite bow paddler's side eddy turn

After using the eddy as a resting area or river scouting location, we perform what is known as a peel out to re-enter the downstream, moving water.

A **peel out** is the reverse of an eddy turn in many ways. To perform a peel out, the paddlers give their canoe some forward momentum to successfully free themselves of the eddy. The canoe is angled between 30 and 45 degrees, or up to 90 degrees for a sharp turn, from upstream in the direction the paddlers wish to turn. When peeling out, the river team paddlers *lean downstream* to prevent the rushing water from causing their canoe to capsize. Like the eddy turn, the turning direction relative to the bow paddler's paddling side will dictate the stroke combination used - either a bow Duffek stroke and stern forward sweep or a bow cross draw sweep and stern reverse sweep into a low brace. Paddlers should plan a peel out according to river strength, their paddling abilities, and impending paddling needs.

Figure 173. Building up speed to peel out

Figure 174. Peel out to bow paddler's paddling side

Figure 175. Re-entering moving water

Figure 176. Peel out illustration

We now have skills for controlling the craft during ferrying across the river and for making our way into and out of eddies. Let's now look at the last of the basic river skills we will be learning: **shooting the rapids**. *Remember, for our standard stationary strokes to be effective, the canoe must be moving faster than the river's current.*

Figure 177. Shooting the rapids

The challenge in shooting the rapids is recognizing and avoiding river obstacles. Paddlers find the most successful method for shooting the rapids to be *proper scouting* of the river *before entering* the rapids and *successful reading* of the river *while in* the rapids. Paddlers cannot always spot every obstacle, so the team must be prepared with the ability to quickly maneuver the canoe. Here is where our flat water sideslipping drills become valuable. The bow paddler calls, "sideslip right!" or "sideslip left!", or maybe just "right!" or "left!", based on his or her assessment of the highest water in which to ride.

Figure 178. Running the river illustration

Remember, the open end of the 'V' marks the points between which the canoe should pass. While shooting the rapids, we employ everything we have learned about canoeing to make our river journey *safe, fun, and exciting!*

Figure 179. Rivers can be safe, fun, and exciting!

River Team Review

1. We recommend safety equipment specific to river paddling in addition to the recommended flat water safety equipment. (a) Name three such items. (b) Can you suggest something not discussed that a river paddler might also find useful during a day on the water?

2. After a river team chooses a river right for them, they often secure the canoe to the roof of a car or truck. List important canoe transport considerations. Try setting a canoe securely for transport using the techniques discussed.

3. What is the difference between scouting the river and reading the river?

4. When scouting and reading the river, the river team's goal is to identify hidden and exposed river obstructions. List five or more river obstructions and describe the water formations associated with each.

5. The river paddler gets into river rider position whenever swimming in moving water. (a) Describe the river rider position. (b) What are some reasons for the river rider position?

6. Capsizing results in both river team paddlers swimming in the river. Prepare now for an unexpected capsize by listing a procedure to be followed if finding oneself in this unexpected situation.

7. Proficient river team paddlers use river power more than paddler power whenever paddling in the river; this is known as working with the moving

Congratulations on your efforts...

Figure 180. Your instructors congratulate you!

water rather than fighting the moving water. Besides working with the moving water when ferrying, the river team should lean the canoe downstream to avoid capsizing. What capsize causing force do we lessen with this downstream lean?

8. Eddy turns are used to successfully enter an eddy. List the bow and stern paddlers' stokes and the procedure for crossing through an eddy line (a) to bow paddler's paddling side, (b) to opposite bow paddler's paddling side.

9. Peel outs are used to exit an eddy and re-enter the downstream moving water. Make two lists for getting the canoe out of an eddy similar to those made for entering an eddy.

10. When shooting the rapids, river team paddlers usually try to paddle in the highest body of flowing water; therefore, (a) experienced river team paddlers would like to shoot through a 'V' with its open end (upstream / downstream). (b) In what situation(s) might the river team not wish to travel with the highest body of flowing water?

Exercise:
    Run a river, which you and your river team partner can comfortably paddle, under the supervision of a qualified river paddler leader.

Bonus:
    Teach others the sport of canoeing to re-enforce the knowledge you have gained through the "*Paddle to Perfection!*" lessons!

...and thank you for helping us throughout our Paddle to Perfection with you!

Figure 181. And we'll all paddle happily ever after...

Index of Figures

Index

Crew Answers

1. **PFD's.** (a) Type II PFDs provide buoyancy and keeps breathing passages clear of water. Type III PFDs provide buoyancy and more movement freedom than Type II PFDs. (b) Unexpected situations could be a boating accident or a person overboard. (see pages 10-11)
2. **Safety equipment.** (a) Extra Line - towing a canoe to safety. Whistle - alerting others of a need for assistance. First aid kit - bandaging a wound or scrape. (see pages 13-14) (b) Two-way communication device - reaching help when no help is within the immediate area. Wool blanket - sudden cold weather.
3. **Nomenclature.** Bow bang plate, bow breast plate, gunnels, bow flotation, bow seat, keel, bilge, deck, bow thwart, midship thwart, stern thwart, stern seat, stern flotation, stern breast plate, stern bang plate. (see page 15)
4. **Choosing a paddle.** 1st method: Place the tip on your shoe, the grip should be between your chin and nose. 2nd method: Curl your fingers around the grip and tip, your arms should be out to the side with elbows straight. (see pages 18-19)
5. **Entering and moving in a canoe.** (a) By stepping across the keel line and "shifting our weight," we keep the canoe balanced and keep ourselves out of the water. (b) Move slowly with both hands on the gunnel to keep body weight low when moving to the seat - or anytime walking in a floating canoe! (see pages 18-19)
6. **Power stroke.** (a) The grip hand makes the power stroke easier by pushing forward. Keeping the control arm straight also makes the power stroke easier. (b) We want the blade to pass vertically through the water to get the most resultant forward momentum possible from each stroke; a blade not passing vertically through the water will tend to steer the canoe off course. (see pages 21-22)
7. **Feathering.** (a) The power face in the forward power stroke faces the sky during the forward power stroke feathering whereas (b) the reverse power face faces the sky during the reverse power stroke feathering recovery. (see page 22)
8. **Pivot point.** (a) The pivot point refers to the center of buoyancy or imaginary point where all the upward forces on the canoe from the water could be centered such that the canoe would float in the same position. (b) The pivot point moves toward the heavier end of the canoe; for example, the pivot point would move toward a stern paddler weighing more than the bow paddler. (see pg 25)
9. **Sweeps.** (see pages 25-26).
10. **Cross draw sweep.** The cross draw sweep is merely an extension of the bow paddler's *forward* sweep. (see pages 27-29)

Exercise: Paddling a straight course, stopping, spinning, returning. (See pages 29-31)
To maintain a straight paddling course, the more powerful paddler can:
- slow the rate his or her blade passes through the water
- shorten his or her blade's time in the water
- omit strokes as required
The less powerful paddler can add some forward sweep to the power stroke.

Captain Answers

1. **Captain canoe nomenclature.** (a) cockpit, deck, bilge, ribs, floats.
   (b) length, beam, draft, freeboard. (see pages 33-34)

2. **Knots.** square knot: securing gear to the thwarts; sheet bend: extending an anchor line; bowline: making a temporary dock line. (see pages 35-37)

3. **Safe capsize and rescue drills.** (a) capsize drill: Stow paddles, move to canoe middle, curl knees over gunnel, place inside hand on gunnel opposite legs, lean canoe, slowly fill canoe with water. (see page 40)   (b) No available help: • Swamped canoe swim • Capistrano flip (see pages 41 and 44)   (c) Canoe-over-canoe rescue procedure: beam-to-end, rescue positions, hoist canoe so gunnels rest on gunnels, roll and return canoe to water, re-enter canoe, check physical conditions, collect gear. (see pages 42-43)

4. **Changing paddling positions.** (a) Paddlers change paddling positions to learn both bow and stern strokes. (b) The leapfrog method keeps the center of gravity <u>low</u>. (see pages 45-46)

5. **J-stroke.** (a) The <u>stern</u> paddler uses the J-stroke. (b) The *pitch*-J is used for slight course adjustments. (c) The *hook*-J is used for large course adjustments. (see pages 47-48)

6. **Moveable strokes.**
   (a)   pushaway or moveable pry
   (b)   moveable draw
   (c)   pushaway,
   (d)   moveable draw
   (see pages 48-53)

7. **Stationary strokes.**
   (a)   stationary pry
   (b)   stationary draw
   (c)   stationary pry,
   (d)   stationary draw
   (see pages 54-57)

8. **Stationary cross-draw.**
   (a)   the stationary cross draw is like the *stationary pry*
   (b)   only the *bow paddler* uses the stationary cross draw
   (c)   approximately 30° (typically between 15° and 45°)
   (see pages 56-57)

9. **High and low braces.**
   (a)   The power face pushes on the water during the <u>high brace</u>.
   (b)   The power face pushes on the water during the <u>low brace</u>.
   (c)   The paddler essentially must be part of the canoe for the high or low brace to result in righting a leaning canoe. (see page 58)

10. **Duffek stroke.** The Duffek Stroke combines the <u>stationary draw, high brace, moveable draw toward bow, and forward power stroke</u>. (see pages 59-60)

Solo Answers

1. **Canoe construction materials.** Canoe construction materials affect a canoe's resistance to sand and abrasion, resistance to denting, quietness in water, weight, ease of repair, and cost. Since canoe construction materials continue to change, we recommend researching which canoe construction materials provide the qualities you desire by speaking with experienced paddlers, canoe shops, and canoe manufacturers. (see page 62)
2. **Rolling hitch.** The rolling hitch tends not to <u>slip</u> once on a pole. (see page 62)
3. **Solo portaging.** (a) The leg walk is useful for short distance carries. (b) Clever solo paddlers team up and perform a two-person two-canoe breast plate carry. (see pages 63-64)
4. **Solo positioning.** The solo paddler would move toward the bow when paddling directly into the wind. (see pages 64-65)
5. **Reducing paddling energy.** (a) The canoe tends to bear away from the paddling side so using the wind to counteract the canoe's tendency will limit need for the J-stroke. (b) Moving toward the bow will reduce the canoe's tendency to turn away from the paddling side. Moving toward the stern will reduce the canoe's tendency to turn toward the paddling side. Adjusting weight accordingly makes the solo paddler's stroke more efficient because the need for a compensating stroke, like a forward sweep or J-stroke, will be reduced. (see page 64-66)
6. **Solo C-stroke / J-stroke.** The C-stroke first steers the bow toward the paddling side then away from the paddling side. The net result is the canoe's going straight. A normal power stroke will require more of a hook-J and results in a slow startup. The C-stroke combines a moveable draw, power stroke, and J-stroke. (see pages 67-68)
7. **Outside pivot turn.** In solo paddling, the solo paddler generally sits directly above the canoe's pivot point (assuming no relatively heavy gear rests elsewhere in the canoe). The 180° sweep, therefore, rotates the paddle around the pivot point. A 90° sweep when solo paddling would only use half of the possible sweep stroke area. (see pages 68-69)
8. **Inside pivot turn.** (a) The inside pivot stroke combines a reverse sweep and a sweeping draw stroke toward the bow. (b) The paddler slices the blade through the water to get the blade back to starting position. (see page 69)
9. **Sculling strokes.** The sculling versions of the moveable strokes are more graceful than those requiring an 'in-the-water' or 'out-of-water' recovery. The sculling strokes are also very efficient since the blade is continuously applying the stroke. (see pages 69-70)
10. **Solo Duffek stroke.** Leaning <u>into</u> the turn aids the paddler in turning the canoe when using the Duffek stroke. (see pages 69-70)

Exercise: While paddling through the obstacle course, one should be conscious of extending the length of each stroke, positioning weight to reduce need for pitch J-strokes, maintaining forward momentum through turns, and working with the canoe rather than *muscling* the canoe through the water. (see page 70)

River Team Answers

1. **Safety equipment.** (a) Rescue bag, wetsuit or drysuit, helmet. (b) Waterproof flashlight, arrival schedule for transportation members. (see pages 72-74)

2. **Transporting a canoe.** Important considerations for canoe transport are sturdy roof racks, strength rating on car attachment points, strap and line strength ratings, driver visibility, and local transport laws. (see pages 75-77)

3. **Scouting the river versus reading the river.** Scouting the river is performed *on the river bank prior to paddling* a river section; reading the river is performed *on the river while paddling* a river section. Using both skills is important for safety on even well known sections of river. (see pages 78-79)

4. **River obstructions.** (a) big rocks beneath water's surface: standing waves - mounds of water which appear not to move. (b) big rock just below water's surface: pillow - smooth, dark water surrounded by rushing water. (c) large branch or tree limb: strainer - almost no change to water flow. (swimmers will not pass through and are likely to be forced underwater; often causes fatality) (d) large volume of water passing over a big rock into sudden drop off: hole - water curling back on itself in circular motion. (e) rocks between which to paddle: 'V' with open end upstream - rough, fast water forming a chute. (see pages 80-82)

5. **River rider position.** (a) Float on back facing downstream with feet at the water's surface. A swimming paddler uses the river rider position to keep feet and legs from being trapped beneath below-water river obstructions and to fend off above-water river obstructions. (see pages 82-84)

6. **Capsize procedure.** River teams should, before paddling, discuss their unexpected capsize procedure. Procedure: (a) save yourself (b) get into river rider position (c) count heads (d) move to the upstream end of the canoe (e) get to the river bank (f) check physical conditions (g) collect gear (h) change into dry clothing if necessary (see page 84)

7. **Leaning downstream.** The capsize-causing force reduced by leaning downstream is the water undercutting the canoe, which tries to roll the canoe to the upstream side. (see pages 85-86)

8. **Eddy turns.** (a) eddy turns to bow paddler's paddling side: bow - duffek stroke into power strokes; stern - stationary draw into forward sweeps into power strokes. (b) eddy turns to opposite bow paddler's paddling side: bow - stationary cross draw into power strokes; stern - reverse sweep into a low brace into forward power strokes. Apply strokes after the bow has crossed the eddy line at an angle between 30 and 45 degrees. (see pages 86-89)

9. **Peel outs.** (a) peel out to bow paddler's paddling side: bow - Duffek stroke into forward power strokes; stern - forward sweeps into forward power strokes. (b) peel out to opposite bow paddler's paddling side: bow - stationary cross draw into forward power strokes; stern - reverse sweep into a low brace into forward power strokes. (see pages 89-91)

10. **Shooting the rapids.** (a) A 'V' with its open end *upstream* is generally an indication of a safe paddling line. (b) One situation when travelling with the highest body of flowing water would not be desirable is when the rough water would be too overpowering for an open canoe to navigate. (see pages 92-93)

Robert Tannenbaum, Photographer
Black and white photographs
Front cover white water photograph

Amy L. Solomon, Photographer
Front cover flat water photograph

Gary & Mark Solomon

Gary and Mark Solomon founded Aquatics Unlimited in 1989. Aquatics Unlimited is a watersport education organization which offers hands-on training in rowing, canoeing, kayaking, waterskiing, windsurfing, and sailing. Both Mark and Gary earned four instructorships and ten other certifications through the American Red Cross. After many years of teaching children from the ages eight through fifteen, Gary and Mark began Aquatics Unlimited to train American Camping Association affiliated camp waterfront staffs and have been involved with adult education programs.

International Scale of River Difficulty *

Moving Water Classifications

Class A: Water flowing under two miles per hour.
Class B: Water flowing two to four miles per hour.
Class C: Water flowing greater than four miles per hour.

White Water Classifications

Class 1:
Easy. Fast moving water with riffles and small waves. Few obstructions, all obvious and easily missed with little training. Risk to swimmers is slight; self-rescue is easy.

Class II: Novice
Straightforward rapids with wide, clear channels which are evident without scouting. Occasional maneuvering may be required, but rocks and medium sized waves are easily missed by trained paddlers. Swimmers are seldom injured and group assistance, while helpful, is seldom needed.

Class III: Intermediate
Rapids with moderate, irregular waves which may be difficult to avoid and which can swamp an open canoe. Complex maneuvers in fast current and good boat control in tight waves or strainers may be present, but are easily avoided. Strong eddies and powerful current effects can be found, particularly on large-volume rivers. Scouting is advisable for inexperienced parties. Injuries while swimming are rare; self rescue is usually easy but group assistance may be required to avoid long swims.

Class IV: Advanced
Intense, powerful but predictable rapids requiring precise boat handling in turbulent water. Depending on the character of the river, it may feature large, unavoidable waves and holes or constricted passages demanding fast maneuvers under pressure. A fast, reliable eddy turn may be needed to initiate maneuvers, scout rapids, or rest. Rapids may require "must" moves about dangerous hazards. Scouting is necessary the first time down. Risk of injury to swimmers is only moderate to high, and water conditions may make self-rescue difficult. Group assistance for rescue is often essential, but requires practiced skills. A strong eskimo roll (for kayakers) is highly recommended.

Class V: Expert
Extremely long, obstructed, or very violent rapids which expose a paddler to above average endangerment. Drops may contain large, unavoidable waves and holes or steep, congested chutes with complex, demanding routes. Rapids may continue for long distances between pools, demanding a high level of fitness. What eddies exist may be small, turbulent, or difficult to reach. At the high end of the scale, several of these factors may be combined. Scouting is mandatory, but often difficult. Swims are dangerous, and rescue is difficult, even for experts. A very reliable eskimo roll (for kayakers), proper equipment, extensive experience, and practiced rescue skills are essential for survival.

Class VI: Extreme
One grade more difficult than Class V. These runs often exemplify the extremes of difficulty, unpredictablilty, and danger. The consequences of errors are very severe and rescue may be impossible. For teams of experts only, at favorable water levels, after close personal inspection and taking all precautions. This does *not* represent drops thought to be unrunnable, but may include rapids which are only occasionally run.

* *Used with permission of the White Water Affiliation, Phoenicia, NY.*

skill sheet

Crew

- [ ] safety
- [ ] use of PFD
- [ ] safety equipment
- [ ] nomenclature
- [ ] choosing a paddle
- [ ] portaging
- [ ] boarding & deboarding
- [ ] using the paddle
- [ ] forward power stroke
- [ ] reverse power stroke
- [ ] feathering
- [ ] stopping the canoe
- [ ] turning mechanics
- [ ] forward sweep
- [ ] reverse sweep
- [ ] compensating strokes

Captain

- [ ] nomenclature
- [ ] physical dimensions
- [ ] care of equipment
- [ ] square knot
- [ ] sheet bend
- [ ] bowline
- [ ] portaging
- [ ] capsizing & self rescue
- [ ] canoe-over-canoe rescue
- [ ] Capistrano flip
- [ ] switching positions
- [ ] J-stroke
- [ ] moveable strokes
- [ ] stationary strokes
- [ ] high and low braces
- [ ] tandem Duffek stroke

Solo

- [ ] canoe materials
- [ ] rolling hitch
- [ ] solo portaging
- [ ] seating locations
- [ ] C-stroke & J-stroke
- [ ] inside pivot turn
- [ ] outside pivot turn
- [ ] moveable strokes
- [ ] stationary strokes
- [ ] solo Duffek stroke

River Team

- [ ] river equipment
- [ ] transporting the canoe
- [ ] knots for canoe transport
- [ ] selecting the river
- [ ] reading the river
- [ ] scouting the river
- [ ] river obstructions
- [ ] swimming the river
- [ ] river capsizing
- [ ] ferrying
- [ ] eddy turns
- [ ] peel outs
- [ ] shooting the rapids
- [ ] running the river